CN00940443

Burnham-on-Sea

BRIDGWATER
The Parrett's Mouth

Poems by James Crowden

Photographs by Pauline Rook

AGRE

In memory of all river pilots and those involved in commercial shipping up and down the tidal reaches of the River Parrett as well as all fishermen, hobblers and mudhorsemen.

First published in 2000
by AGRE BOOKS
Groom's Cottage, Nettlecombe,
Bridport, Dorset, DT6 3SS

www.agrebooks.co.uk

All rights reserved. No part of this book may be reproduced in any form
or by any means without permission in writing from the publisher,
except by a reviewer who may quote brief passages in a review.

Copyright © 2000 text James Crowden
Copyright © 2000 photographs Pauline Rook

The authors have asserted their moral rights

Typeset and printed in the British Isles
by Bigwood & Staple,
Bridgwater, Somerset

ISBN 0 9538000 1 6

A CIP catalogue record for this book
is available from the British Library

Contents

Acknowledgements

OUR biggest thanks must go to the Mayor Roger Lavers, and the Charter Trustees (pictured opposite), whose financial support was an enormous help. We would also like to thank the following: Chris Sidaway for his advice and support through Sedgemoor Arts, South West Arts for a publishing grant which helped set up Agre Books, Louise Hurrell and Charlie Dearden of Bridgwater Arts Centre who initially approached Pauline Rook with the idea of commissioning a special photographic exhibition, staff at Bigwood & Staple for all their skill, patience and hard work in the design, reprographic and print departments, Stuart Brill and Senate for cover design, Katie Curtis for the map, Jonathan Hudston for his keen and constant editorial input and Sara Hudston for expert guidance in many areas.

Our thanks also to all those who have let us photograph them on their farms or in their factories. We got a marvellous response, people's willingness to help was enormous, and this made the project very enjoyable. Some photographs were not at all easy, others just 'happened'. We've found Bridgwater to be a fascinating and diverse place. It's like towns used to be, lively, up front, and quirky. We would like to thank Gill Slocombe, the Vagabond Carnival Club based at The Commercial Inn, Redgate Street, Dave Perris of Rice's Farm, Cannington Grain & Cannington College, Alan Sparkes of Perry Court Farm, the Darbys of Middlezoy, Bob Heard of Westonzoyland, Bill Chedgey of Bridgwater, the Rt. Hon. Tom King CH MP, The Somerset Willow Company, UCB, Jonathan Dethier of Spindlewood, Cricket Malherbie Farms, Federal Moghul, The Somerset Brick & Tile Museum, Admiral Blake Museum, Bridgwater Library, Hinkley Point, Brian Hubbard, Thompsons, Peter Lee, Robin Prowse, Keith Budden, Nigel Hector, Robin Thorn, HM Plant, Brendan Sellick and Les Pople. For photographic help and encouragement Ron Frampton FRPS and Jessops for materials.

For historical information we have relied mainly on the critical abilities of Dr Robert Dunning as well as the breadth and depth of the Victoria History. About the docks, well-researched information is available from Brian Murless in his various publications and papers, particularly the one on slime batches. Roger Evans' books have also added a rich vein of local colour to the town's history. Rod Fitzhugh's collection of old photographs gives a deep insight into the scale and diversity of the river trade.

Bridgwater is endlessly fascinating whether you are looking at Civil War politics, nonconformity, rebellion, shipping, or heavy industry. We hope that we have done justice to the people, the town and its history, and that Bridgwater will survive the next 800 years.

James Crowden & Pauline Rook

A NOTE on the Charter Trustees: The first three charters granted by King John in the year 1200 really set Bridgwater going as a town and inland port. Further charters followed, the last in 1835 was only superseded by local government reorganisation in 1974. These days the Charter Trustees are made up of Sedgemoor district councillors elected to represent the Bridgwater wards of Bower, Sydenham, Quantocks, Eastover, Victoria and Hamp. From their number they elect a Mayor annually.

In the photograph – Seated from left to right: John Turner JP, ex-British Cellophane & TGWU; Jennifer Briscombe, ex-British Cellophane; David Busby JP, ex-British Airways cargo management; Roger Lavers, Hinkley Point mechanical engineer & Mayor 1999-2000; Mick Briscombe JP, engineer & full-time officer of the AEU; Sandy Buchanan JP, lecturer, author & industrial archaeologist; Adrian Moore, ex-British Cellophane & British Rail. Standing left to right: Gill Slocombe, heavily involved in the carnival & library service; Brian Gillard, ex-senior traffic warden; Julian Taylor, social worker, part-time lecturer & woodturner; Philip Smeed, ex-police superintendent; Brian Smedley, van driver, rock musician, playwright & author of a booklet on the Brick Yard Strike; Cyril Avent, ex-schoolteacher & ornithologist; and Kathy Pearce who worked at the Royal Ordnance Factory. Unfortunately Bill Monteith, engineer, engine driver and computer wizard, and Ken Richards, who worked in the brickyards man and boy, were both absent for the photograph.

Introduction

IN its heyday Bridgwater was the Hong Kong of Somerset, bustling with a rich mixture of entrepreneurs and traders, free thinkers, nonconformists, translators and inventors. The port was far more complex, colourful and cosmopolitan than it might at first appear and its legacy lives on. In a sense, all of Somerset still flows through Bridgwater.

Inland ports are a rare and much neglected part of our social history. They played a vital part in commerce and formed the nerve centre of every county. Bridgwater's port was part of a trade network connecting Somerset with Ireland, Barbados, Canada, the Baltic, Jamaica, Italy, Spain, Norway and Russia, France and the East Indies. At one time the town boasted seven shipyards and had consuls from Germany and Sweden. Wool and wine were of great importance, as were woad, iron and coal, sheep and cattle, grain, millstones, timber, cider and beans. Jewish bankers, Florentine merchants and Flemish weavers, plus any number of goldsmiths, silversmiths, dyers, tuckers, fullers and carders, helped build enough prosperity to support two medieval hospitals, and a friary.

All this trade relied on the river. To understand Bridgwater fully, you have to appreciate the idiosyncrasies of the River Parrett and its tidal mouth; the oddities of coastline and estuary, the shining mudflats, the bore, floods and shifting sandbanks, the migration of geese, eels and salmon, the flow of history and commerce, the chronicles of navigation, pilotage and shipping, wrecks and groundings, the need to maintain causeways and crossing points, quays, bridges and wharfs. The Parrett is a powerful, unpredictable river, whose once navigable tributaries, the Tone, the Isle, the Yeo, the Cary and the Brue, lead far into rich farmland, the soft rich green underbelly of Somerset, a flat, sinuous landscape, riddled with rhines.

In these days of juggernauts, high-speed railways, air freight, satellite communication and container ships it is almost impossible to understand how important coastal shipping once was. The tug of wind on taut canvas, the smell of salt water so familiar to generations of crews; rough and ready men, filled with a sense of exploration and adventure – all this is lost and with it the knowledge of porterage, tonnage, keels, masts, sails, cordage, charts, caulking and ship's chandlers.

In 1086 the Domesday Book referred to Bridgwater as *Brugie*. The inhabitants paid tax for five hides, had ten ploughs and were subservient to the North Petherton Hundred which had a fine hunting forest and attracted royalty. At this time the manor was held by Walter of Douai, who probably gave Bridgwater half its name. Even today, if you listen closely, the town name sounds just like Brigewaltier. The 'bridge' part comes from the Norse *bryggja*, meaning quay or jetty.

Walter's estate was large and parts of it around Bridgwater later passed to a Devon landowner, William Brewer, who was a great friend and hunting companion of King John. At Chinon near Tours, on 26 June 1200 King John rewarded Brewer's loyalty by granting him three charters, effectively giving him permission to build a castle and a bridge. More importantly the King gave the town itself free borough status. This relieved its people of serfdom and enabled the burgesses to trade freely with the rest of the country and administer most of their own affairs. In other words, it was a radical shift away from

feudalism. As a free port, the town was able to expand rapidly, and become part of the European trade network. King John also gave permission for markets and fairs to be held in Bridgwater, a concession which still survives today, as do the Charter Trustees, who still meet to discuss and decide matters of local importance. More charters were issued in 1318, 1371, 1381 and 1400. By the 15th century Bridgwater had become a busy port and strategic centre. Complete self-government came in a charter of 1468, which conferred the right to elect a Mayor.

The tide of history has left its mark on the town. Robert Blake, General and Admiral, scourge of the Dutch and founder of the modern British navy, was born in Bridgwater in 1598. During the English Civil War Bridgwater endured a memorable siege and Monmouth's doomed army met its fate nearby. The bloody justice of Judge Jeffreys was meted out at hangings, dismemberments and mass deportations.

In the 18th century the town created great wealth. Castle Street (pictured above) was one of the finest Georgian streets in Somerset. Construction began in 1723 on the orders of the Duke of Chandos. The architect was Benjamin Holloway, who used the proceeds and perhaps some of the materials to build himself a fine residence known as the Lion's House, just round the corner from Castle Street.

It seems an appropriate moment, 800 years after the granting of the first charters, to take a contemporary look at Bridgwater. This book seeks to capture the essence of this diverse industrial town, as well as the countryside surrounding the tidal reaches of the River Parrett. Black and white photography is a fitting and exacting medium for a place with Bridgwater's gritty and hard-working history. I hope my words do it justice.

James Crowden

Carnival Girl

One lone girl
And 17,000 light bulbs
Dancing the night away
Up front on the Vagabonds' cart

Minutes before the start
An eerie silence

Ahead, the waiting crowds
Lining the streets, twenty deep,
The November night
A little cold for a bare midriff

Her last job, putting lipstick on the men.

Yawn

Painting and testing
No sleep for days –
A gang of thirty or more
Have drawn the carnival cart from its shed
Like the first airship, with inches to spare.
After the secrecy, the clandestine clubs and the meetings,
The long hours and the days raising money,
Bedecked and dazzled like Tribal chiefs
The men strut and preen their feathers,
Flutter like Birds of Paradise,
New Guinea and the Amazon Rain Forest
Condensed into a single night
A foreign army of Masai warriors, Egyptian priests,
School teachers, witch-doctors and medieval courtiers
Buddhist monks, saddhus and go-go dancers.
The religion of light and phantasy
A Festival of colour, spectacle and sacrifice.
Heroes for an evening, glitter of stage
A folk drama, a passion, a medieval pageant
That keeps the world revolving for another year.

Harvest Below High Water

While ships belt on up to Dunball Wharf,
There's a locust hard at work on the sea's acre,
On the big-headed Equinox, the short-strawed
    wheat
Behind the sea wall, which gave in once
And drowned 1200 pigs, on the other side.
Beware the nor'wester on a spring tide.

Cannington Grain

Vast silos hover, belly down and interconnected,
Like some gigantic Space station, landscape
From another Galaxy. Five hundred acres
Compressed into a single bin behind the maize.
Enormous reservoirs of solar energy,
Heavy industry, farming the sky, the staff of life.

Mobile Dairy – Westonzoyland

Keen eye of the dog, udders in good shape
A bit of grub and the vacuum pump
Fresh air, cleaner than a normal parlour
Doors slam, *Next please.*

The last of the summer settlers,
Nomadic herds beneath the open sky,
The summer pastures, rich and verdant
Wisdom of Impermanence, a Somerset solution,

An independent spirit that came unstuck
By Bussex Rhine, the other side of the village
Night surprise, an early pistol shot.
The Monmouth Rebellion crushed before breakfast,

Gaffer Scott's Vagabonds cut down in the corn,
Swinging from trees, like hams
Hung, drawn and quartered, boiled in brine,
"Ten years in Barbados. *Next please*".

A cushy little number by comparison.
Sugar cane instead of cheese, a package tour,
And still spoken, a few choice dialect words
Lodged there in the Caribbean, milking history.

Cannington College

Shearing sheep, deceptively easy
When you see it done well. Determination
And hard graft, the learning curve of balance,
Long hours in the shearing shed.

There's nothing quite like it
For working up an honest thirst.
Everyone should have a go, from top to bottom,
Back to nature, sweat, dung and lanolin.

The Suffolk no doubt has the upper hand,
As does the Lord Chancellor sitting on his woolsack.
All that economic history, ornate church towers
Woven cloth, the golden fleece and golden hoof.

But when eventually you get it right,
And the handpiece flies through the wool
Of its own accord, you forget about shearing,
The whole world is suddenly at your feet.

Bridgwater Fair

Lot 61

What am I bid? *What am I bid?*
Come on now gentlemen
Let's make it brisk
Farming's in a terrible mess
You never had it so bad
Come on now Gentlemen
Dig deep in your pockets
Twenty Suffolk Cross, two tooths
Look fine on your farm
Well bred, well bred, broad in the beam
Who'll give me 20?
15 . . . 15 it is,
Lady's bid on the left
17.50 . . . 20 . . . 22.50,
25 . . . 27.50
Who'll give me 30 . . . 30 . . . 30 . . .
32.50 . . . 35 . . . 35 . . . 35 . . . all finished
I sell to the Mayor at 35 pound a head
Look fine on your farm Sir
Lawn big enough?

Lot 62, same farm
Who'll give me 30?

Fair Gain

Gypsy boy and gypsy pony
Both tethered to the open road,
A knack of shifting on,
Ingrained in a twinkling,

Restlessness harnessed up.
Beneath motorway bridges
They tell each other's fortunes,
In caravans read the tea leaves

Thumb through newspapers,
The small print at the back,
Boning up on the world price,
Aluminium, lead and copper

The range of mobile phones
And Transit vans,
Scrap metal and tarmac –
Never put down too many roots.

No doubt you will see it all at Priddy Fair,
Riding bareback through the crowds,
Making good, and looking with a keen eye
For the lucky eye of each passer-by...

Bob Heard

Fuller on Spaxton church bench end

The Great Mace

Worked silver, a symbol of power
And office, the town's coat of arms
Bridging Commonwealth and Restoration
A time of purity and letting rip

After the fortunes of War,
The siege which saw Christabella
Try and pull a fast one on Cromwell,
The pot shot from the ramparts,

The Royalist taunts, her dress undone.
No doubt Charles remembered well
The warmth of his wet nurse.
Who by all accounts passed beyond

The normal bounds of duty.
The great mace dedicated to his affection
A memento of hotter moments –
When great tides flowed beneath the bridge.

East Quay Updraught Kiln

Small loaves of red brick once fed this hungry
    town.
An oast house, a beehive, a vast bread oven
Round and tapered, bolstered, braced, squat and
    firm –
The kiln sits on its haunches, door into another
    world.

Hard labour, the black mouth, the grate,
Coal-fired and shovelled the steady updraught,
Cannily fed and intricate with flues, hot air and
    flame.
Safely cloned, red suburban skyline, streets
    ahead.

Bridgwater Reclaimed

Stacked up in composite heaps
Single Romans, Double Romans,
   Triple Romans
Pan tiles, Finials, Triple Angulars,
Scallops, Clubs, Plain and Ziggurat

Weatherblock and Bargeboard
Waterbar and Hurricane, Fishscale and
   Homestead
Wineglass Paragon, Lockjaw and Marseille –
Acres of roof running wild, miles of tiles.

British Cellophane That Was

Across the allotments, avenues
Of neatly planted lettuces and leeks
Leading to the shrine of cellophane
The latest thing in the nineteen-thirties.
Men only too willing to work there
After the second war, escaping the drudgery of the land
And battlefields, fleets of bicycles parked up,

As if L.S. Lowry was waiting for them
To go home on the stroke of four.
A lifetime of packaging and chemical reactions –
The smell is better than it used to be. UCB NFB
Now cling-film and black plastic bin bags.
In the cemetery to the right
A Sergeant who charged with the Light Brigade.

High Altitude Willow

Like enormous Christmas hampers,
Balloon baskets rise gently from the floor,
Two a week, tough and supple, ideal for flight,
Hot air tugging at their cargo, seductive, the bird's eye view,
The lackadaisical drift over landscape,
Known and yet only half known, remote farms,
Villages without name, rivers and woods.
Then the moment of uncertainty, an eye on the weather,
The sudden fall from grace, the gravity of the situation.

During the war half the town was at it,
Supply drops parachuted in behind enemy lines,
Wicker baskets complete with suggestive notes
From the Bridgwater girls, the Home Front slipped in.
Now it's dog baskets for the Royal Corgis
Bread baskets for Richard Branson and Virgin Atlantic.
Willow coffins at the back of the shed,
Ecology, green burials, very fashionable these days.
Resurrection for the next Millennium an optional extra . . .

Spindlewood, Bridgwater

Making goats cheese at Nether Stowey

Pistons In Colley Lane

From small ships to aircraft
Compressors to motorbikes
High speed, high performance
Aluminium alloy, tough and light
Cast, then turned down to the nearest 'thou'

This is the hard-nosed business
That put working horses out to grass
And changed our roads and fields forever.
Each lathe shedding silver strands of swarf,
Each fine wisp, oil cooled.

It all hinges on compression, strength and agility
The tail end of the Industrial Revolution
Revolving day and night, the chuck
World-wide precision engineering,
The beast, that must be fed and tamed.

Inside Hinkley Point

Abstract sculpture conducting steam
From high to low pressure,
Temperatures that would make your hair
Stand on end, and a lot else.

Contortions like the guts of a dragon
Or an ageing battleship, lagged and insulated
Silver piping forms its own contours –
The reassuring whine of high speed turbines.

A massive pressure cooker, Somerset's sauna
Fuelled by Einstein's mathematics,
Monitored by Russell's logic, a political move
At the height of the Cold War. *Some Like It Hot*.

Burnham-On-Sea

Halfway between sloth and meditation
The sun cure, a mild form of intoxication –
Time and tide cease to matter
When sea and sand are close to hand.

The languid flavour of the English relaxing,
In their own rather flaccid, placid way
As if permission is needed from the harbour master
To show an extra inch of skin or leg.

Coded space and childhood memories,
Charted out with deckchairs and sandcastles
Windbreaks, the inevitable lack of glamour
England's passport to democracy.

Kilve Beach

The squall whipping in a Turner sky,
Trouble over Bridgwater Bay.
Between Steep Holm and Burnham
Dragon's bite, by-passing Brean
Terraced slabs – what's left of the dragon's teeth
Where congers lurk, glatting at low tide
With terriers and sticks, slithering back to the sea.
Each promontory a defiant cliff

And round the snubbed nosed corner
Out of sight, the real dragon lies doggo
Tucked away in its lair.
Puffing gently to itself,
Nuclear power, quietly biding its time
Harnessed with horoscopes
Steam coming out of its massive ears,
Its belly full of uranium and half lives.

Aisholt

A slender fore arm
Encircling the village,
Tight grazing and early lambs,
The sward, rich reservoir in summer.
Hemmed in neatly, hugs the narrow lane
Of church, house and tree.

But now the land, naked, smooth and free
Reassuring in its completeness
And pared down to the bone,
Flexes its muscles, fold by fold.
Nature, taut like a bowstring,
Resonates within, to its own tune.

Quantock Trees

Trees and the reflection of trees,
Sharp shadows heeled into hedges
Low, winter light lancing the fields
As if a river of grass was flowing uphill.

Timber and memory awakened
Saunter along arm in arm,
As the sun's orchestra sweeps up
Above the kindling ridge.

Caught between branches
A perfect negative, leaves behind
Only itself, a shallow haunting,
Dancing the light fantastic.

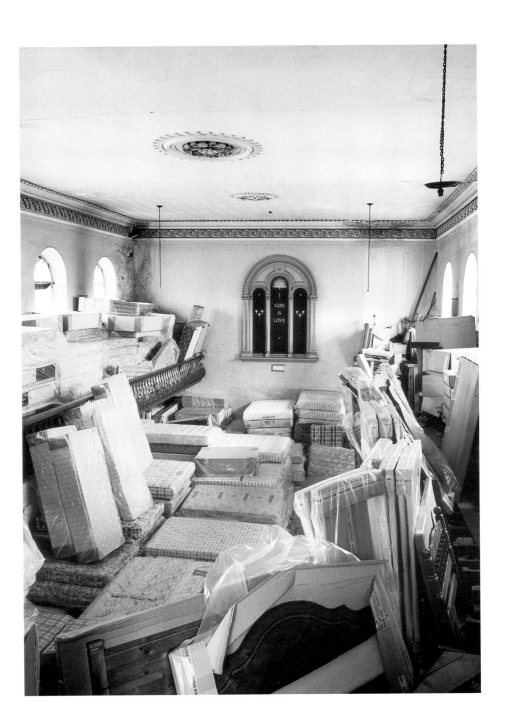

Mattresses In The Wesleyan Chapel

The Nunc Dimittis: Love Is God

Dissent and Nonconformity, a Bridgwater trademark
The Creed, the spirit of lawlessness preserved.
A birthright, pushing the boundaries out
To the very edge, the rough and smooth
Absolution, walking on the muddy waters
The idiosyncratic river, which like the Ganges
Or the Brahmaputra runs through their daily lives
Baptism by Carnival and high tide.

These mattresses have stories yet to tell
a voyage of discovery.

Let us pray for all those whose bodies shall lie thereon
And wish them well on Saturday nights,
In the life hereafter, in countless bedrooms
Scenes of nakedness and passion yielding,
Hope springs Eternal, the night's messengers,
Lust, love and pillow talk, face to face,
And then exhausted collapse into the arms of sleep,
Adam and Eve bedding down once more in Somerset.

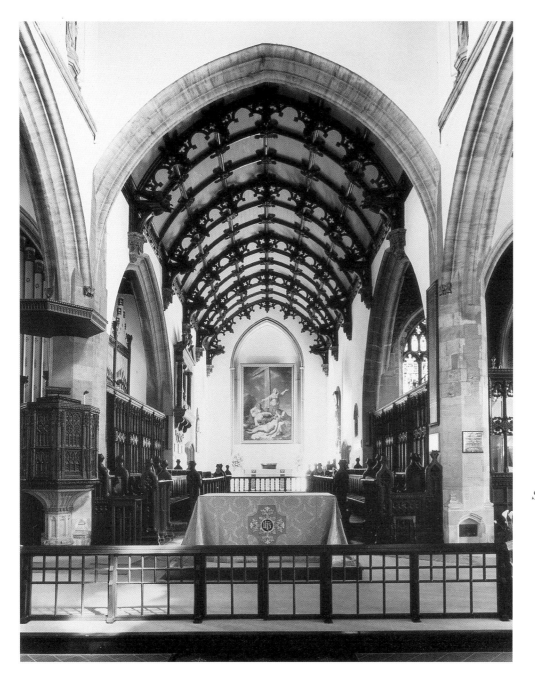

St Mary's church, Bridgwater

Angel Place, Bridgwater

Ironmongers

Two centuries of kitchen clutter,
Egg timers, scales and gas masks
By Royal Appointment
Carpet beaters, oilcans
Knife grinders and mincers
Put through it everyday
The House of Windsor
Overseeing every bill and invoice.
Ironmongery and knick-knacks
The patent medicine,
Paraphernalia preserved,
A haven of oddity hibernating.

Town Bridge

Linking two worlds, Eastover and Westover
Two banks, a causeway, a crossing point
Between two tribes, Bristol & West
A place of off-loading, slips and quays
Of hobblers and barges
Mooring ropes, bores and trows,
The river tamed, hemmed in, abutted
A house for salmon, eels and elvers,
A focal point, for assignations
With shopping baskets and the tide,
The ebb and flow of the opposite sex,
Daily life, a ripple in the sunlight
A span, a toll, a rib, a riveted arch,
Through which all of Somerset flows,
For better or worse, richer or poorer
Mud, salt, wool and wine, brick and tile
A human cargo, Chartered since King John, .
A place of security, a port, a castle, a watergate
A thin thread crossing the Parrett's mouth.

Bill Chedgey

My father, one of twelve, was a miller, a bit of a bare knuckle fighter he was, Jess Chedgey, but his professional name was Jack Armstrong... two of his brothers were killed in the First World War so he kept his head down and then ran a pub for forty years, *The Ship Afloat*, a tough but interesting place, full of rough characters, brickyard workers, dockers, sailors. It was a cider pub and Acker Bilk used to slip in to whet his whistle after performing at the Town Hall. The population of Bridgwater was 17,000 and there was 120 pubs. Well that's one extended family a pub, but they weren't all pubs as you'd understand it today, the women would do the brewing and open up their front room in the evening... I ended up in the Post Office, but when war came I joined the RASC. In 1942 we became a special parachute unit, held in reserve and then sent to southern Italy, near Bari. The wicker baskets we dropped were made in Bridgwater like us, and the girls back home would put little messages in with their addresses, *Dear Tommy etc etc love Brenda*, well I didn't dare reply, you see I was married and if word got around there'd be another war... But then eventually they dropped us at Arnhem with gliders... course I got out alive, but only just...

Landed on the Monday, got captured on the Sunday morning, so we had six days of it. I was in the second wave. The last day we were in the top floor of a house and the Dutch family were down below with the kids, I had a bit of an 88 shell in my leg, nearly took the leg off, broke the femur anyway. I told the others to get back while I hauled myself downstairs. It's funny you don't feel pain at that stage...

I got to the open door and lay on the door mat on my back and realised that I still had Phosphorus grenades on me and if they were hit I'd go up with them, because you can't put them out, so I threw them down the street and the other Mills bombs I had and then I passed out, you see we hadn't had any sleep or food for three days... I came to and as I looked up under the rim of my helmet I realised I was looking into the mouth of a Schmeiser. There were four German-speaking soldiers, two German and two Dutch, they were only teenagers, they gave me the half grain of my own morphine and then carried me to a dressing station on a blanket. You see I only got sent to Arnhem because a friend of mine had broken his collar bone...

After the war I went back to the Post Office and became an inspector of postmen and then Mayor... Local history and tapes for the blind is what interests me now...

Rt. Hon. Tom King CH MP

Caught outside the dentists,
Where King Square meets the top of Castle Street,
Tom has represented Bridgwater and the Quantocks,
Countless stags and pumping engines, odd corners of the Levels
And thirty miles of coastline for thirty years.

No doubt he would have defended the town
In time of Civil War, but which side
Would have had his loyalty then?

Now he's Chief of some Joint Intelligence Security Committee
Which means he is supposed to know
What's going on in MI5 and MI6 and GCHQ.
Spying on the spies, elvering in Chinatown.
But even if you do know, mum's the word.

Robin Prowse, bird warden

Spoonbill and eel on Stogursey
church bench end

Peter Lee, river pilot

Keith, elver dealer

Net Income

Parked up like hundreds of others,
A young lad with an elver net,
Smuggling the night away,
A piratical attitude licensed under moonlight,
Stakes his claim on the early morning.
River run, high, wide, full and fast,
Pushing in, on top of the spring tide,
A rite of passage, a moment of peace.

Elvers at the end of their long sea voyage
Fresh from the Sargasso,
The Mystery of Creation
Hoicked from the river's darkness,
Wriggling filaments' migration,
Translucent, pale and gelatinous.
They talk of kilos and cash on the nail,
Caribbean currency courtesy of the Gulf Stream.

Dodington Copper Mine

Sprouting out of the infra-red barley
The ruins of an engine house
Whose scalding steam once pumped
The mine's water to surface,
The oscillating Cornish beam
Essential for mining copper ore,
Smelted and cast into bronze and brass,
Molten liquid squeezed from the foundry
Nails for ship's hulls, church bells, chandeliers.

But for the humble charcoal burner
Nestling under Quantock, little comfort –
A meagre living scraped from the hillside,
The skill of slow burning, night and day
Under turf, slender billets of oak,
Smoke rising from ancient stories,
Of promiscuity and good looks.
Wilful wifely murder, the trial
A caged gibbet that creaks in the wind.

Approaching Combwich at 8½ knots

Combwich Pill

Tales From The Riverbank

Spiling, a simple solution,
The watercourse way, weaving willow
Between stout posts, green engineering
A living barrier taking root
Curbing the winter water's wrath
An angry animal, fluid and fluctuating,

The river's energy dissipated and deflected,
Deep pools that once devoured meadows.
Undercut banks, tamed and ameliorated,
Sent on its way seaward, humbled.
A protector of ox-bows and bends,
Beefs itself up year by year.

Tidal Lock

Each dock gate a massive barn door,
Tall as a small house
Braced, pivoted and overgrown
Entrance to the Tidal Basin
Opening onto the river, the sea beyond,
A cascade of nautical journeys,
The Baltic, Canada and Bordeaux,
Scandinavia, East and West Indies,
Cardiff, Ireland and Bristol
Genoa, Germany, Spain and Portugal

All once squeezed through here
With timber, coal, steel and cotton,
Feedcake, maize, sand and cattle,
Vessels that slowly shed their cargo,
With hooks, chains and steam cranes,
Gang planks, hawsers and lighters.
The harbour door still ajar
The silt, a fine sediment at its foot
Jammed and wedged, a powerful reminder –
The river still means business.

Thorny Solution

A bicycle made for three
Unchains the days
Along the towpath
The wheels of life careering
Where heavy horses
Once heaved heavy barges
The smell of navvies' sweat
Hung in the hedgerow,
And the echo of hooves
Faded into the distant haze.

Brendan Sellick

Three generations out on the mud,
Pulling the fish, cod, bass and whiting,
Skate, eel, plaice and shark
Yes the sea is good to us . . .
Grandfather he once caught a ninety pound sturgeon
And then there's the shrimps,
Hundreds of years my family been fishing here

Letting the wind run through the nets
You never know what you'll find,
But you got to watch the tide and the mud
It comes in faster than you can ever imagine,
And with the sledge, you've got to keep pushing it
Otherwise you sink in, and that would be that.
We don't have no radar or wireless or sonar,

Just hundreds of years of staying alive
But you still got to carry the fish back to the shore
And that's half a mile or more over your shoulder,
Adrian works nights at the jam factory
And Cain is still at school
All the other mud fishermen gave up, but I stuck it out
The sea's in our blood, salt water in the veins.

Les Pople

I have been fishing this river since 1953, and I am now 76. We used to get a lot of salmon here, just nosing their way in. I worked as dock foreman at Dunball for many years, sometimes I seen six ships on one bend, four going up and two going down . . . that's in Marchant's Reach.

My house is just by the old barrage balloon hanger . . . of course they were trying to get Bristol during the war but sometimes they dropped bombs on the way back. Just before I joined up I saw a Heinkel brought down. It crashed just two fields away from ROF, the explosives factory at Puriton. If that had gone up, we'd have gone as well, and Bridgwater probably. I saw the five parachutes come out, they rounded them up pretty quick, but they never twigged that the Huntspill was the reservoir for the factory, they needed a lot of water for making explosive, still do.

But this year they only let us fish for three months, from June 1st to the end of August. We used to get May as well but they never reduced our licence fee. So far we've only had five salmon this year. We pay £55 for fifty butts, or putchers as others call them. I got two sets, one at Dachoots and one on Marchant's Reach. Bob Thorne he used to keep his out at Black Rock. But there's very few salmon around now, one year we got a hundred. If we see them caught on the sand we get the flatners out and go for them in the moonlight, sometimes if you are not down quick enough, the foxes get them or the crows. The tide, he goes out pretty quick, you got to be fit, why a man got caught in his nets up Monmouth way and drowned the other year, the slop here, that's the fine mud, that builds up on the neaps and then gets washed out on the springs, some places I can walk across the river, but if you get it wrong you've had it, the banks keep changing, particularly in winter.

The flatner you see got a flat bottom hence its name, and it's good for sliding down the mud to the water, any other boat the keel $\longrightarrow$

would sink in and get stuck. They are about sixteen foot long, but some are nineteen foot. You've got to have a good bit of bank to get them down, where there's no rock, then you can go dipping with a round net and follow the salmon, but there's no telling where he'll come up. A dip net licence used to be ten shillings, now it's the same as the butts. Then you got to get the boat back up the bank when the tide comes in, the lighter the better. Modern ones are made of fibreglass now. As for salmon, I carry them home on a bicycle. I once had three; a nineteen-pounder, a fifteen-pounder, and a ten-pounder. That's quite a weight, you should try it uphill. I got several 'S' hooks, but I use a ladies' bike, the paint work don't matter so much.

Once a tanker damaged sixteen of my putchers, they didn't believe me, but I followed the tanker up to the wharf and there were two still hanging on with bailer netting by the intake pipe for the cooling water. They couldn't argue after that . . .

I use metal ones now, but when we started it was withy, they take the pressure of the tide, the front stakes are elm. Hell of a strong they are, they got to have that give in them, and the putchers they get narrower. We used to have round ones, but I prefer the square ones, less gap between them. But the salmon, once they're in the trap they don't swim out, they can't turn round but they're quite happy sitting there, they got no option, a salmon can't reverse. But the tide and the silt eventually get them though through the gills. It's muddy water all right but one year we had heavy rain all May and the water was clear, we had acres of salmon then. Ninety-nine we got that year. You see they're Atlantic salmon pushing on up the Severn. They nose in just to check the water, but it's usually their last and only mistake. If we get tags we send them back. I like to see a flash of silver in the butts, or the flapping of a tail . . . then we get on down quick, before he swims out . . . Sometimes we get dead cats, dogs, ferrets, foxes . . . All get trapped in there. It's amazing what the flood water brings on down. My real fear is getting babies.

My son helps me now, but I don't think I'll be doing it another year, I had a heart bypass last year . . . just thought I would keep it going till the end of the century . . .

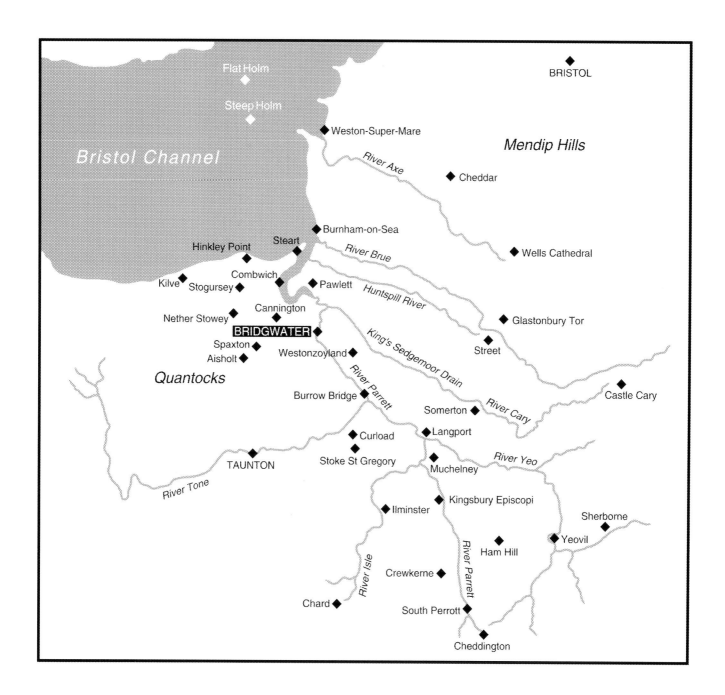

Notes

Castle Street: Castle Street is now the domain of dentists, doctors, accountants, solicitors, an arts centre and a nursing home. In nearby Queen Street there is a curious, 'modern' building, Castle House. This was built in 1851 by the Akerman family who were keen to demonstrate the building properties of pre-cast concrete and post-tensioned concrete in mock-Gothic style. It's the world's oldest concrete building and is sadly very neglected. Bridgwater Arts Centre, the first of its kind outside London, opened in 1946. A year later it hosted an international symposium on modernist architecture attended by the architects Le Corbusier, Maxwell Fry and Walter Gropius. No doubt the re-building of Europe was on their minds. Concrete proposals!

Carnival: If Bridgwater is famous for one thing, it is the carnival now held every year on the Saturday nearest November 5. The procession is often more than two miles long and crowds can exceed 120,000. Each club is centred on a particular pub and members spend all year raising about £25,000, enough to buy a flat or a small house. Cash collected on the night goes to charity.

In the old days, the carts were horsedrawn and the tableaux more like Old Master oil paintings, full of colour and dignity. One problem with horsedrawn carts, however, was that local lads would throw firecrackers and startle the horses. Nowadays most of the carts owe more to Hollywood than Rembrandt. They are powered by lorry engines or tractors and pull behind them vast generators pumping out enough electricity for a medium-sized village. This year the Vagabonds chose *Viva Brasil* as their theme. The girl pictured here, Hayley Edwards, was about to dance in front of the cart for at least two hours. Competition between clubs is very fierce and every point makes a difference when the judges are roving around.

Symbolically it is the cleansing of the old year, Halloween, a riotous community celebration after harvest – in atmosphere rather like the tar barrel racing in Ottery St Mary in Devon. Instead of flaming barrels, Bridgwater has squibs, like large roman candles mounted on a wooden pole and held in the air. These fireworks produce a spectacular display outside the Town Hall. Regulations have had to be brought in about the size of squibs – in the past some people who've let them off in pubs have been dumped in the river or hauled up in front of the magistrates. Perhaps it's no coincidence that only a few miles away is the Royal Ordnance Factory at Puriton which specialises in experimenting with new explosives . . .

Harvest Below High Water: This field is called Henry Trick's and it's one of the last in the parish of Wembdon, near Stallington's Clyse where Cannington Brook flows into the Parrett. The field belongs to Dave Perris of Rice's Farm, Cannington, and in his own words Dave farms "full blast". We found him in his yard filling up his muckspreader at top speed and no sooner did he appreciate we were not officials, than the kettle went on the Aga and he began to talk:

"That field with the combine in, is well below high water. A little disconcerting when it's lapping your wellies and the field is four feet below. One hundred acres of cereals and that particular field had wheat in it the year before and now has barley. Wheat, wheat, barley, beans. Maybe just over three tons to the acre. Equinox, and the contractor Steve Perry from Westonzoyland. The ground tends to crack up a bit where the tramlines were and Yes there is a few wild oats in the distance . . . but forget those. The river forms a big loop here. The day the sea wall came down was the day before Victoria was born – 17/12/81 – and she's a tall girl now . . . It was worst the other side. Steart had it bad too. One farmer up there thought they'd had it. The power was off and suddenly three feet of water appeared in their sitting room, the road was cut off and the waves buffeting them on all sides. It seemed like they was an island cast adrift and floating out to sea. Dave Perris had seaweed all on his field. Some people have to pay for that privilege," he chuckled.

"I was the first to plough that field. All the ditches and hedges were cleared by Italian prisoners of war, they were laid back and glad to be out of it, the Germans were a bit more serious. But in summer, particularly on the other side at Pawlett Hams they were always short of water, and in the nineteenth century Lord de Morley bought two fields this side and then laid a pipe under the river and had the water pumped up to his rhines by windpower. It worked well and even supplied drinking water to several farms in Strecholt. But that's foreign over there. Been to America but never been to Pawlett Hams or Wales for that matter."

Cannington Grain: These silos, about half a mile out of Cannington on the Combwich Road, take grain from a large area. Cannington Grain Store Ltd, a farmers' co-operative, was formed in 1977 with thirty-five producers and storage for 5,000 tons. Now there are over 700 producers and they handle approximately 120,000 tons with affiliated depots in Cullompton, Bodmin and Saltash. In the old days grain went out from ports such as Dunball, Watchet and Falmouth, but now it's more likely to be Avonmouth or Southampton. Most of the grain is feed wheat and goes for animal feeds. At the peak of the harvest they accept 2,000 tons a day. The grain is cleaned, dried and graded.

Just down the road we talked to another cereal farmer, Alan Sparkes of Perry Court Farm, Wembdon, who's not only on the drainage board, but something of a local historian. It was a real pleasure and education to listen to him talking about the land, the Bronze Age flints and high quality Roman pottery he'd found. The Romans grew grain around here and could export it where they needed it. There was a port at Crandon Bridge and another at Combwich. Some of the most interesting things Alan showed us were old drainage board maps with historic parish boundaries, revealing several places where the river has changed course over the years. Bits of Chilton Trinity and Wembdon are now on the 'other side'. Ox bows had been cut through and an old river course filled in. The river is always on the move, indeed it's so windy it was once said to be 'as crooked as a barrow pig piddling in the snow'.

Mobile Dairy – Westonzoyland: The sight of mobile dairies, or milking bails as they are called in Somerset, is increasingly rare. This one belongs to the Darbys of Chapel Farm, Middlezoy, and was photographed in a field called Lang's. Sometimes in summer they move the dairy twice a week. This is much more hygienic than trying to keep a concrete dairy sterilised with gallons of chemicals. The Darbys have a herd of seventy-two cows and the two sons Christopher and Paul do most of the milking now. The future is uncertain. A very particular and individual way of life is at stake.

Cannington College: Learning to shear sheep is one of the hardest jobs on the farm, but one of the most rewarding when you get the knack. Here the student has just taken a break from shearing a large Suffolk ewe. It can often take you half an hour to do what a Kiwi will do in a couple of minutes. Unfortunately the price of wool has dropped over the last decade and the wool which once paid for the shepherd's wages now barely covers the cost of the shearing. Wool was a staple raw material in the Middle Ages and finely woven cloth commanded a premium price. Now with central heating, acrylic sweaters, and indoor lifestyles, sheep are left mostly to serve as providers of roast lamb and mutton curry, as lawnmowers, and as cosmetic additions to the countryside. Though O.P. sheep dips have tainted that bucolic image.

As for Cannington College, it caters for a wide range of students, young and old, and is extremely good and versatile. Originally it was a Saxon Manor which later became a Priory for Benedictine Nuns and a refuge for Somerset gentry's wayward daughters. These young ladies needed schooling, but it may well have been the daughters who ended up leading the nuns astray... An inquiry in 1351 revealed that nuns had been misbehaving with chaplains in the nave of the Priory church and there were a few more children than there should have been. Cannington Court was later owned for many years by the Clifford family. The main hall is still called the Clifford Hall. There are seven walled gardens and ten greenhouses. Also nearby is Brymore, a very successful state-funded boarding/agricultural school.

Three men watching a Shetland pony being sold at Bridgwater Fair

Bridgwater Fair: King John's charters in 1200 declared Bridgwater to be a Free Borough, so the town was able to levy tolls on outsiders. It could also stage weekly markets and an annual fair. First, there was an eight-day fair beginning on Midsummer's Day, June 24. This survived until 1359. No doubt the Black Death contributed to its decline. But another fair was established in 1404 and confirmed by a new Charter in 1613. This also lasted eight days, and started on St Matthew's Day, September 21. These days it starts on the last Wednesday in September and lasts for four days. There used to be round-ups of ponies on Quantock, but they became too rowdy and it could be dangerous driving wild horses through crowded streets. Nor should we forget that fairs in the past were an important source of employment where many a farmworker would hope to be hired for another twelvemonth. Today we are commercially spoilt by out-of-town shopping, credit cards and the internet. But it is good to see livestock still being sold and there's always the bright lights of the funfair. And I think it's a healthy sign that farmers' markets are on the increase – people like to buy direct from source.

Bob Heard: In the 1850s Bob's great-grandfather Robert Heard walked up from Beaford in North Devon to take an engineer's job at Westonzoyland Pumping Station. On the way he got married!

Bob's grandfather Walter John took over a Westonzoyland pub called *The Three Greyhounds* (now known as *The Sedgemoor Inn*) and ran it from 1882 to 1913. He also made a wise move when he bought a MacLaren and then a Burrell 7HP Traction engine for £500 in 1905. Walter also invested in a Foden threshing machine, which Bob still keeps in his barn. Looming behind Bob in our photograph is the trusser bought in 1918 to work with that threshing machine. The Heards would often be out threshing from September to Easter. Nowadays Bob, who's retired, likes to take the machine round to shows. The Burrell traction engine, incidentally, went on to pull out timber near Langport.

Fuller On Spaxton Bench End: This photograph shows a fuller with yards of cloth using a fuller's double-handled wooden hammer, which was used with fuller's earth for cleaning and thickening cloth. Fuller's earth came from Combe Down near Bath. Various types of cloth were made, called serge, kerseys, Taunton's, Chard's and Bridgwater's. Most were twelve yards long. Teasels were used to bring up the nap. Some cloth, like the Penistons made in Wiveliscombe, was blue and hard-wearing, a bit like denim. It was shipped out to the West Indies for clothing slaves, they would each get six yards at Christmas.

The Great Mace: Bridgwater's famous silver includes a Charles I salt cellar dated 1638. This very fine mace was made in 1653, during the English Commonwealth, by a silversmith in Ludgate Hill for £25 11s 6d. At the Restoration the town thought it best to forget the Commonwealth, so they fixed on a Royal crown, and added the inscription: "Charles II King of England, Scotland, France and Ireland 1660". The references to Christabella Wyndham allude to events during the siege of Bridgwater in July 1645 when Royalists were trapped inside the castle. The spirited wife of Colonel Wyndham stood on the ramparts and took a pot shot at Cromwell, missed and killed his ADC. How different British – and Irish – history would have been if she'd succeeded. Cromwell had already only just survived being drowned in the Parrett when his boat was overturned by the bore.

Christabella had been wet nurse to the future Charles II, and later during the siege reputedly showed off her breasts to a Roundhead messenger, thus making very upfront her intention not to surrender. A few days on, before the castle was finally stormed, she escaped during a temporary truce to the continent via the Isles of Scilly and Jersey. Historical gossip suggests that Christabella slept with the king-to-be on his fifteenth birthday (29 May 1645) in Bridgwater Castle itself. Royal education, loyal subject.

Bricks, Tiles & Kilns: From the early 18th century Bridgwater and its surrounding river basin became increasingly famous for producing bricks and tiles. Many of the old clay pits are now flooded and they provide urban havens for wildfowl and fishermen. As the pits were dug, the clay changed colour. Best for tiles was the middle batch of grey clay. Beneath that came the blue clay which mixed with upper light brown clay would make bricks. The brick kilns were simpler than the more sophisticated pottery and tile kilns, but still required ingenuity to get an even firing. Tile kilns would be fired for four days and then left to cool for four days. Each firing produced about 5,000 tiles and used about ten tons of coal. In 1861, eight million bricks were made and by 1900 this had risen to seventeen million, most of which were exported.

Mention should be made of the so-called 'Bath' scouring brick made from river silt collected in shelves (called slime batches) on the riverbank. The rate of slime deposition was reckoned to be about twelve feet a year. So, periodically, the batches would be shovelled out, and the slime carried away in barrows to be put in a pug mill, extruded, moulded, stamped, dried and then fired. Some say the bricks were named after a Mr Bath, others maintain they were simply the same colour as Bath Stone. They were used to provide a fine abrasive powder which, when mixed with water or soda, was used for cleaning metal work, fenders, knives, floors, tables, etc. Only at certain points a mile or so up and downstream of Bridgwater was the tidal slime of the right consistency of very fine particles of silica and alumina. The slime was

Sydenham Manor, inside the British Cellophane works

also used for sealing the entrances to the brick and tile kilns during firing.

In the trade's heyday, Bath bricks were sent to Europe and America, even to China. Modern soap and detergents, plus the power of advertising, killed off this peculiar but lucrative business. It was such a good earner that works' owners consistently prevented attempts to improve the Parrett's drainage. They wanted their raw material to keep coming free of charge, and any improvements to the river would have meant removing their precious slime batches.

Thousands were employed and inevitably there were several strikes about the pitiful pay and long working hours. During one notorious strike in 1896 troops had to be fetched from as far away as Plymouth. The Riot Act was read outside the Town Hall and soldiers with fixed bayonets charged the crowd. Wages and conditions eventually improved, but brick and tile workers remained at the mercy of diseases like pneumonia and silicosis.

The last firing in Barham's brickyard at East Quay in Bridgwater was in 1965, and the last surviving kiln is there. The yard's now the Somerset Brick & Tile working museum, normally open to pre-booked visitors on Thursdays and Fridays during the summer.

Our photograph was taken at Bridgwater Reclamation in Monmouth St.

British Cellophane: Courtaulds' arrival in 1938 cured the unemployment left by the decline in the brick and tile works. Over 2,500 people were employed here, with another 1,000 in subsidiary firms like Bonded Fibre

Fabrics, which makes J-Cloths and jacket linings. Linked in with this, Bridgwater had a tradition of shirt and collar making with Van Heusen, now closed.

Cellulose is in fact a natural product derived from eucalyptus woodpulp shipped in from South Africa.

The Sergeant who rode into the Valley of Death in the Crimean War in 1854 was Sgt. Denis Heron. Severely wounded in the arm, he was nursed by Florence Nightingale herself. He died in 1895.

Another rich piece of history is Sydenham Manor (see the photograph opposite), which is tucked away inside British Cellophane. Richard Percival, brought up there, not only published the first English-Spanish dictionary, he used his expertise to translate and decode captured Armada plans in 1586, which delayed Spanish invasion plans for a couple of years. The Manor house is now very sedate and is used as a conference and training centre.

High Altitude Willow: The Somerset Willow Company run by Aubrey and Darrell Hill is based on The Wireworks Estate in Bristol Road, Bridgwater. It's a thriving innovative business employing more than a dozen people. The firm's main claim to fame isn't the Corgis, or Sir Richard Branson, but the balloon baskets made for Cameron Balloons of Bristol. Working with willow is a skilled and exacting task, but as a material its strength and suppleness is unmatched. The Hills buy their willow from the Derham family of North Curry. There's a good company website at www.somersetwillow.co.uk.

Spindlewood: This woodturning business is another fine example of a small enterprise flourishing in Bridgwater. Set up by Jonathan Dethier eighteen years ago, Spindlewood occupies The Old Bakery in Edward St. The picture shows Richard Ellis with a heavy-duty gouge working on a twelve foot column of Douglas Fir destined for Hampton Court Palace. The original column, much decayed since the 1680s, was designed by Sir Christopher Wren, and was sent down as a model for Spindlewood to work from. Other recent Spindlewood creations have included a four poster bed for Chicago, a staircase for Caithness and a fine array of candlesticks, knobs and chair-legs.

Of Men And Cheese: At Cricket Malherbie Farms Ltd in Nether Stowey, the four men cheddaring the curd are (from left to right) Anthony Villis, Mark Webb, Terry Touchin and Patrick Villis. Each one of the firm's stainless steel vats holds about a ton of cheese. Annual goats' cheese production is about 200 tons. Currently made for St Helen's Farm, it's available in most supermarkets. Other Cricket Malherbie dairy products include about a thousand tons a year of own-brand cheddar cheese, as well as butter, yoghurt, and sheep's cheese.

Pistons In Colley Lane: Federal Moghul cast and finish pistons for high performance engines. We visited the factory during a heatwave and the management had issued ice creams to all the staff, which we thought was a very humane gesture. Colley Lane is also the likely site of Bridgwater's earlier foundry which cast ploughs for farmers, various church bells in the 18th century, and even cannon for privateers. There was iron in the Brendons, copper in the Quantocks, tin in Cornwall, lead in the Mendips and coal in Wales.

Inside Hinkley Point: This is the steam turbine hall inside Hinkley B where all manner of pipes conduct steam and water to and from the vast turbines that actually generate the electricity. Though I am not a great fan of nuclear energy I am impressed by the scale of the beast, and can admire the sculptural technology that's gone into its design. The reference to Einstein concerns his crucial matter into energy equation ($e = mc^2$), the reference to Bertrand Russell relates to *The Principles of Mathematics* (1903), linking maths with logic, without which binary mathematics and modern computing would not be possible. Hinkley A, closed down at the time of writing, was set up in the fifties as a 'bomb' factory, and in its day was the largest of its kind. *Some Like It Hot* is of course a reference to Marilyn Monroe who was dallying with the President around the time of the Cuba Crisis back in 1962.

Burnham-on-Sea: This is the true Parrett's Mouth and the final bend in the river can be seen in the middle distance, as can the mudflats and sandbanks that make navigation a major problem. This photograph looks as though it was taken in the 1950s and has that general old-fashioned air which adds to the charm of England's seaside resorts. The two girls, Mary and Alice Rook, are eating ice cream from Styles on Exmoor.

Kilve Beach: This blue lias beach fascinates geologists, shelving as it does in spectacular patterns, which leave behind great rock pools where at low tide congers lurk. The sport of catching congers (known locally as glatting) used to add excitement to the foreshore. Men with dogs and long sticks would go hunting them.

The other extraordinary thing about this beach is the attempt to set up an oil shale industry here in the 1920s. A railway from Bridgwater was planned to help exploit the find, but nothing came of it, although a retort for extraction still stands and the reserves are still there. In the Twenties it was one of the largest discoveries of its kind in the world. Also there is an old lime kiln. Hinkley Point lies round the corner – a rampant red dragon is after all the symbol of Somerset. In the distance you can see the island of Steep Holm.

Aisholt & Quantock Trees: Quantock villages are renowned for their tucked-away, delightful eccentricity. Samuel Taylor Coleridge, William Wordsworth and his sister Dorothy explored the area when they lived at Nether Stowey and Alfoxden in the late 1790s, and it stimulated some of their greatest work (eg 'Kubla Khan'). Coleridge considered renting a cottage in Aisholt in 1800, but it was deemed too remote. Aisholt was the Quantock home of the Blake family, and also a bolt-hole for the poet Sir Henry Newbolt (1862-1938): "Drake he's in his hammock an' a thousand miles away . . . Slung atween the round shot in Nombre Dios Bay" ('Drake's Drum'). These early morning photographs are, I think, outstanding.

Mattresses And Nonconformity: Bridgwater has strong Nonconformist traditions. The Puritans first held meetings in the town as early as 1592. The Baptists date back to 1630. Numbers swelled during the Civil War and by 1669 there at least seven other different groups, including Presbyterians, Separatists, Congregationalists and Quakers, some of whom had come in search of sanctuary from less tolerant parishes. Not that they always found it; in 1683 militia-men forced their way into the Quakers' circular meeting house, then burnt its pulpit and pews on the Cornhill. Members were put under house arrest. In the 18th century, the great Methodist preacher John Wesley visited Bridgwater six times. This photograph shows the inside of the Wesleyan Chapel in King St. Built in 1816, it only ceased being a chapel in 1978. Other establishments remain in use; there's the Unitarian church of 1688, with a fine shell porch in Dampiet St, where Coleridge preached in 1797, and the vast neo-classical Baptist church built in 1837.

One group worthy of particular mention is a religious sect which moved to Spaxton in 1846. The Agapemone, or 'Abode of Love' as it was called, was packed full of wealthy good-looking young women under the spell of their 'Messiah, Lord & Master', a Mr Prince who would ride into Bridgwater in an open-top carriage pulled by four large bays, complete with outriders in purple livery and a pack of bloodhounds. As if this wasn't enough to draw attention to himself, in 1856 the Messiah deflowered a sixteen-year-old virgin called Zoe, naked in front of a congregation including his own wife, as the organ played. The altar was apparently a billiard table. This was called The Great Manifestation, and needless to say it caused more than a bit of gossip in Bridgwater. The girl became pregnant, and the Messiah's halo slipped a little . . . but the community was liked. At its peak members numbered 200, and their charity and spending power was welcomed by the villagers of Spaxton and the tradesmen of Bridgwater. Mr Prince died in 1899 but a successor was found and the 'Abode of Love' continued. Numbers dwindled, however, and the house was sold in 1958. It makes the 'hippy' communes of the 1960s seem tame by comparison.

As to the mattresses, they are in great demand. The business is run by Brian Hubbard. Recently, though, a FOR SALE sign was seen on the side of the building.

Diggers made by Fiat Hitachi, imported by HM Plant, Bridgwater,
and distributed from here across the UK

Maybe it will, after all, be converted into bijou residences . . .

St Mary's, Bridgwater: The town's main church is mostly kept locked, unfortunately. The painting behind the altar, 'Descent from the Cross', was given to St Mary's in 1780 by Lord Anne Pawlett of Hinton St George (he was called Anne after his godmother Queen Anne). The painting was a prize from a captured Spanish ship, and it dates from the second half of the 17th century. Sir Joshua Reynolds would always stop and look at it when he passed through on the stagecoach. The pulpit and the screen behind the choirstalls are both medieval, while the ornate Corporation screen is Jacobean. Robert Blake was baptised at the font in 1598 and the ill-fated Duke of Monmouth used the church tower to spy out Royalist troops before the Battle of Sedgemoor.

Angel Place: Aptly named after the church and the chapel. This is the new face of the new religion, retail therapy. Instead of priests there are customer advisers, instead of sidesmen, there are security guards. You park on top, in heaven, and shop below, where instead of an altar, there's a mobile shrine, the lift, and only seats for the chosen few. The collection of course goes into the till.

Ironmongers: Living perhaps in a different age, this is the office of Thompsons, the well-known Bridgwater firm founded in 1797 and still going strong. Their original shop was compulsorily purchased for a shopping precinct in 1982 and they are now based near the Sedgemoor Splash. The office is a rare shrine to eccentricity, a living museum. At one time the business employed twenty-two people including plumbers, blacksmiths, copper-smiths, tin-smiths, bell fitters, brass workers, key cutters and even ship's chandlers. They also sold their own shotgun cartridges, firebacks from Ironbridge and all manner of sports equipment. The royal portraits go back to George III.

Town Bridge: This particular bridge was erected in 1883. It replaced a very fine 1797 iron bridge built in Coalbrookdale and shipped down the Severn in sections.

Prior to this was the medieval town bridge, known sometimes as the Great Bridge, which was originally built in 1200 by William Brewer, then improved in the 1390s by John Trivet. Large ships could not get through the Great Bridge, so while the castle was still in existence all goods were taxed through its water gate, which still exists as an alleyway on West Quay. The goods were then re-loaded onto double-ended Parrett Barges operating from what's still known as the Langport Slip. These barges were very manoeuvrable and could ride the bore. Even today when there is a spring tide, and the river is in flood, water will almost touch the top of the arch of the Town Bridge.

Other bridges of note in Bridgwater are the Black or Telescopic Bridge, which used to carry a railway and could be retracted for shipping; the Bascule Bridge in the docks; countless very fine red brick canal bridges; and the two rather plain but functional concrete road bridges. The Bristol & West Building Society have been in

Bridgwater for thirty years. Their premises used to be a pub called *The Punch Bowl*.

Bill Chedgey: His father's pub *The Ship Afloat* was well remembered by Brendan Sellick. A good old cider house. Kingston Black, Bridgwater Pippin and Golden Knob are local varieties of apple, which were no doubt popular with sailors. Apples and cider were useful for preventing scurvy on long sea voyages... and on land!

Rt. Hon. Tom King CH MP: We met Tom in the Bridgwater Conservative Party HQ opposite the Police Station and Magistrates Court, which seemed appropriate as far as Law & Order was concerned. Tom's thirty years in Bridgwater have been eventful and he once fought three elections in four years. His other jobs have included being Secretary of State for the Environment, Transport, and Employment, all in 1983. Then Secretary of State for Northern Ireland 1985-89 and Defence 1989-92. In 2000 he announced he was going to retire from Parliament at the next General Election.

Whilst on the subject of politics, it is worth recording the famous Bridgwater by-election of 17 November 1938 when Vernon Bartlett, a prominent journalist who had worked for The League of Nations, stood against the Conservative Patrick Heathcoat-Amory. The vote was of national importance, as it was fought on the contentious issue of Chamberlain's appeasement of Hitler. Bartlett won by 2,200 votes, Britain went on to re-arm, and as another more distant result of the late 1930s furore over the fate of Czechoslovakia, Bridgwater now has a thriving Czech/Slovak Friendship Society, set up in 1990, led locally by Brian Smedley. For more information see *November 17: The Bridgwater Czech/Slovak Link* by Brian Smedley, published by the Friendship Society in 1999.

Bird Warden: Robin Prowse has been English Nature's bird warden at Steart since January 1979. He's pictured at the top of his new observation tower. Robin's main responsibility is to monitor migrant bird populations in Bridgwater Bay Reserve, set up in 1954. Many species over-winter here as they do in other parts of the Severn estuary and Somerset Wetlands. There are lapwing, dunlin, redshank, greenshank, black tailed godwit, curlew, plover, knot, teal, shelduck and Canada geese, to name but a few. In April, Robin walks out across the mud in the mouth of the Parrett to Steart Island, which was once inhabited and used for grazing. There are the remains of ancient fish traps out there, a small house and stories of ale and loose living when boats got stuck between tides. Robin is also responsible for Shapwick Heath near Westhay. One of his main concerns about living in Steart is the rising sea level. There are mutterings about having to abandon the peninsula. It suffered badly in 1981 and the sea defences are as high as they can be.

Spoonbill And Eel: This fine bench end is from Stogursey church, c.1530. Spoonbills still occasionally turn up today and Brendan Sellick's father used to see them at Stolford. The other birds look like a parrot and a raven. Maybe they are tucking into the Priory grapes. The church has a beautiful brass chandelier made in Bridgwater in 1732, and a medieval sanctuary ring. Hunted villains who touched this won themselves forty days leeway from the law; they would usually wade out to a ship on the next tide. Stogursey also has a fine moated castle.

River Pilot: Master Mariner Peter Lee is Harbour Master at Burnham-on-Sea and it's also his job to pilot vessels up the River Parrett as far as Dunball Wharf. The river bed is always changing and the channel between sandbanks can shift sides in a week. Peter has to regularly walk the river to check the passage is clear. He's written about the changes for an M.Phil. His essay (published in the 1996 Proceedings of the Bristol Naturalists Society) shows that even the deep channels in the bay have been moving, while the offshore Culver Sands have shrunk dramatically in the last fifty years. Peter believes the altered profile of the shoreline has left it more vulnerable to wave damage. Anyway, the average commercial vessel braving the Parrett these days is 1500-2000 tons, with up to fourteen feet draught. There's about fifty-five ships a year though that's set to increase. Cargoes include granite, sand, coal, animal feeds, fertiliser and timber from the Baltic. Then of course, when they've unloaded, boats have to get out again and it's not easy turning them round in a narrow river. Peter has reverted to an ancient technique – shove the bows in a suitable mudbank, let the river do the rest . . . It always works if you judge it right. As you can see from the photograph, at low tide you can almost walk across the river, and cattle sometimes do.

Elver Dealer: For about four months every year, Keith is out on the river bank at all times of the day and night depending on the tide, parked up in a white van. Last year he was visited late at night by two men with black balaclavas and iron bars who stole £2500 in cash. That happened near Moorland. One of Keith's favourite places in the early morning is outside the knicker factory in Huntworth where there's a constant stream of lively ladies going to work on one side of the street, and scruffy, dirty bleary-eyed elver men appearing on the other. As for the elvers, they go up to Gloucester, and then to China, Germany, and Holland, for re-stocking and for eel farms. For several years Keith worked for the eel smokers Brown & Forrest. This portrait of him looking piratical was taken on Burrow Mump.

Net Income: Over the years there's been much debate about the elver problem. Numbers are declining. There are stories in the past of great mats of elvers pushing on up the river, and people coming down through the streets of Bridgwater with buckets to just hoick them out. Often the elvers were fried up in omelettes or sent to Bristol for glue. Sometimes they were just hung up in sacks and used as fertiliser. Nowadays aeration, modern transport, and the price they can fetch, means they are kept alive and looked after. It also means they are prey to over-fishing. Pollution may be another cause of numbers falling, habitats may have been affected by engineering work, and the Gulf Stream may simply have changed its course a little. Indeed, there's some debate about whether eels from Europe ever get back to the Sargasso to breed or whether it's only the east coast American eels that return. Whatever, there's also been a shortage throughout France and northern Spain, so the price is high, though it has come down from the ludicrous heights of £200 a kilo to its normal £40–£60 level, which I personally think is a good thing. Licences cost £32 but the Environment Agency doesn't have the staff to police all the rivers at night. At times the atmosphere down on the river is often very quiet, almost contemplative.

Dodington Copper Mine: To be found just beyond Nether Stowey, this mine was worked from 1712 to 1821 by miners from Cornwall and Derbyshire. It was the only source of copper near to Bridgwater and may well have supplied the bell foundry which existed then. Many of the 18th century church bells of Somerset were cast in Bridgwater. As for the charcoal burner, this refers to the story of John Walford who brutally killed his wife in 1789. Many Bridgwater people went to see him hanged as the trial had been held in their town. Walford's corpse was left swinging in a cage for a year. The tragedy was that he had not been allowed to marry the woman he loved. His story interested Wordsworth and Coleridge, when they lived nearby a decade later. Indeed violence seems to have shadowed the parish. During the Civil War Sir Francis Dodington, the cavalier Lord of the Manor, hanged anyone who surrendered to him. He even shot a priest in Taunton. Today it is very peaceful.

Odd Shipping: In 1878 4,121 vessels made it up the Parrett to Bridgwater. They carried 221,876 tons or an average fifty-four tons a vessel. Today that same total could be carried up to Dunball Wharf in 150 vessels of 1500 tons. Many vessels had problems getting up the river. For example, they might have to queue at places like Marchant's Reach and wait for other ships coming down. If the wind or tide failed, horses and even men were often used to pull vessels up. Many simply went aground and tried on the next tide. The remains of several wrecks can still be seen.

Some historical oddments: During the Commonwealth there was a battleship called *Bridgwater*, she had fifty-eight guns and was built at Deptford. When the Restoration came she was renamed *Anne* and

blown up at Sheerness, one assumes by mistake, in 1673. In 1700 one vessel alone, the *Unity*, took over one million salted herrings to Barbados. Records show that Bridgwater was indirectly involved in the slave trade – but also that the town petitioned Parliament as early as 1785 for the abolition of slavery. In the 19th century, the famous economist Walter Bagehot (from Langport) had a fleet of swift vessels, including five East Indiamen, all registered in Bridgwater. One was called the *Gladstone*. During the last war, there was a sloop called HMS *Bridgwater* and a lend-lease frigate called HMS *Parrett* which was handed back to the US Navy in 1946. In our photograph, the *Union Pluto* is seen carrying granite from Portugal.

Combwich Pill: This was the original port at the mouth of the river, long before Bridgwater existed. It was used by the Romans, who grew corn around here, and had substantial settlements and salt works. There was also a Saxon Herepath or warpath, a hard crossing that gave access at low tide... This was the undoing of a Viking army. Combwich never really stopped being a port, and vessels could off-load coal here between tides. This was faster than going on to Bridgwater, and you could evade the harbour dues. Trade was mainly with Ireland and Wales, the vessels were ketches, schooners and Severn trows. The last known surviving ketch is the *Irene*, built in Bridgwater in 1907, and still afloat!

Smaller rowing boats called flatners were made as well.

The harbour was recently enlarged at great expense to bring in new equipment for Hinkley Point.

Tales From The Riverbank: Spiling is the ancient technique of using stakes and live willow to create a flexible barrier against the current and stop undercutting. It's been perfected by Nigel Hector of Willowbank (and English Hurdle) based at Curload, Stoke St Gregory, and Bridgwater-based consulting engineer Dan Alsop. The riverbank pictured is on the River Axe near Tytherleigh. Interest in Willowbank is growing rapidly. Anglian Water use spiling as part of their efforts to be 'green'. For more information see www.hurdle.co.uk.

The Docks: As a port Bridgwater, like its larger cousin Bristol, had major problems with the tide, narrow rivers and siltation. Vessels moored in the river could only unload at high tide so they often had to be left at odd angles resting on the mud. This meant some cargoes could shift between tides. The solution here as in Bristol was the construction of a floating harbour and wet dock, kept at a constant height. Vessels could lock in and out of it at high tide. Bridgwater's facilities were built by a Devon engineer, Thomas Maddicks, who adapted a sluicing technique used in Bristol for scouring out tidal silt. Maddicks finished the job in 1841 with a little advice from Isambard Kingdom Brunel who was directing work on the new railway nearby. In 1844, Brunel designed the dredger *Bertha*, now the oldest working steam vessel in the UK, if not the world. *Bertha* used to work in Bridgwater. Thomas Maddicks gave up engineering and bought a pub in Taunton. Sadly he died in the workhouse aged eighty-four.

In its heyday in the 19th century the Inner Dock was so full of vessels you could walk from one side to the other without getting your feet wet. One animal feed firm, Bowerings, which has been in Bridgwater for over 200 years, is still in operation, though since the Docks closed in 1971, bulk feedstuffs are now brought in to Dunball Wharf. Bowerings specialise in organic feeds, which go all over the West Country. At one end the docks are also connected to the Bridgwater–Taunton canal, which to this day makes an interesting walk. It's particularly popular with dogs, young lovers and cyclists.

The dock gate photo, like the ones on pages 30 and 66, is infra-red.

Thorny Solution: Robin Thorn and his two children James and Lindsay ride beside the canal at the back of Safeway. Robin came to Bridgwater from Norfolk in 1983, saw the vast regiments of bicycles pouring out of what was then Clarks' shoe factory in Westonzoyland Road, and realised that he'd come to the right place. His business – St John Street Cycles (www.sjscycles.com) – has grown phenomenally. It now employs thirty people. Bikes made and designed by Robin are sent all over the world.

The canal linking Bridgwater with Taunton was completed in 1827. It is interesting to note that a much more daring scheme had been put forward in 1824 by Thomas Telford, who had just completed the Caledonian Canal in Scotland. Telford's idea was to connect the English Channel with the Bristol Channel. Ports were envisaged at Stolford near Hinkley, and under the cliffs at Beer in East Devon. The canal system got as far as Chard and could easily have gone down the Axe valley but the money ran out. Railway mania had taken over. But history hadn't finished with the proposed route. In 1940 it became the Taunton Stop Line and 350 pill boxes were built along it. I wonder which side the Germans would have landed?

Brendan Sellick: Here at the Parrett's mouth, well out into Bridgwater Bay, are three generations of the same family. Brendan is a gold mine of stories and humorous anecdotes. Fishing keeps him fit and in touch with the outside world. Visitors come from far and wide to his remarkable shack at Stolford. In a sense this is Neolithic fishing with poles and nets, just letting the tide do it. There's no diesel fumes, oil slicks, or heavy investment in a fishing boat. At one time there must have been fishermen like Brendan all along the foreshore, but now there's just him. English Nature own the rights these days and issue Brendan's licence. In medieval times fishing rights stretched as far out to sea as the Lord of the Manor could ride on his biggest horse at the lowest tide. At one time, too, there were people called gull yellers who had to shout to stop gulls taking fish from nets. Mudhorsemen are skilled and there are risks if you get stuck or into trouble. The tide comes in at a fair lick. Many of the small hard islands have names, but these never appear on maps – Black Rock, West Winds, Deep Dip, Sandy Bank, West Doors, Conger Ridge, Big Lake, Eel Putts, Bass Path, Flounder Beach, Shrimp Walk.

Les Pople: Eventually caught seven salmon last year. In the old days he could catch that number in a day.

The Heinkel Les remembers was one of three shot down over Somerset in fifteen minutes on 14 August 1940, they were doing a daylight raid on Cardiff.

Bridgwater – the Parrett's Mouth was typeset and printed by Bigwood & Staple of Bridgwater in Monotype Imprint, plus Adobe Myriad on 130 gsm art paper. The photograph above shows Print Supervisor Chris White checking the covers of the book as they are printed on a Solna 525 press. Bigwood & Staple is a long-established family firm with a fine printing tradition, founded by Alfred Bigwood in the mid-nineteenth century. In 1883 Frederick Staple was taken on as an apprentice and by 1894 he had taken over the business which has remained in the Staple family ever since. The press occupies an old grain mill on the banks of the River Parrett in Somerset.

Further Reading

Bridgwater, Robert Dunning (Alan Sutton, 1992)

Squibbs' History of Bridgwater, Phillip J. Squibbs (Phillimore, 1982)

Bridgwater with and without the 'e', Roger Evans (Roger Evans, 1994)

Bridgwater Heroes, Roger Evans (Roger Evans, 1999)

A Quantock Tragedy – The Walford Murder, David Worthy (Friarn Press, 1998)

The Bridgwater Brickyard Strike of 1896, Brian Smedley (1986)

The Bath Brick Industry of Bridgwater, BJ Murless (Journal of the Somerset Industrial Archaeological Society No. 1, 1975, pages 18-28)

Victoria County History of Somerset, vol 6, edited RW Dunning (OUP, 1992)

Somerset: The Complete Guide, Robin Bush (Dovecote Press, 1994)

Somerset, Chris Willoughby (Alan Sutton, 1993)

By Waterway to Taunton, Tony Haskell (Somerset Books, 1994)

Bridgwater and the River Parrett, Rod Fitzhugh (Alan Sutton, 1993)

Bridgwater Docks and the River Parrett, Brian Murless (Somerset County Library, 1983)

In Time of Flood, James Crowden and George Wright (Parrett Trail Partnership, 1996)

www.riverparrett-trail.org.uk A good guide to attractions from the river's source to mouth.

www.bw-carnival.freeserve.co.uk Popular detailed site about Bridgwater Carnival.

www.bridgwatertown.com Official site, includes 3D model of the town.

www.foliot.demon.co.uk/bridgwater.htm Unofficial, enthusiastic view of the town.

www.juniperf.demon.co.uk Another 'unofficial' Bridgwater site. Wide-ranging, opinionated.

About Agre

AGRE Books publishes non-fiction books of literary merit about South West subjects. Based in Dorset, it covers the South West peninsula.

Agre takes its name from the legend of Actaeon and Diana as told in Ovid's *Metamorphoses*. Ovid names Actaeon's hounds and lists their attributes. ''The thicket-searcher Agre'' was the hound with the keenest nose. Agre Books intends to search the thickets of its distinctly rural region to find interesting truths and intriguing stories.

Titles published or forthcoming include:

Islomania by Sara Hudston (£6.50), illustrated with Victorian photographs from the Gibson Archive. Why are people so attracted to islands? Using the Isles of Scilly as its working example, this book explores the special place islands occupy in our imagination.

The Wheal of Hope. Poems and notes by James Crowden, photographs by George Wright. The closure of South Crofty tin mine marked the end of 3,000 years of Cornish history. Wright and Crowden record the last months of the mine and pay tribute to the miners and their heritage.

The Little Commonwealth by Judith Stinton. In the 1910s psychologist Homer Lane opened a remarkable experimental school in a remote Dorset hamlet. Using new material never before published, this account reveals the truth about the community that influenced educational pioneer AS Neill.

To find out more about Agre you can write to Agre Books, Groom's Cottage, Nettlecombe, Bridport, Dorset, DT6 3SS, or visit our website at www.agrebooks.co.uk.

Pauline Rook, ARPS, was born in 1950. She studied food science at Reading University. After getting married, she assisted her husband in the running of a large dairy farm in Somerset for 15 years. Her photographs have been exhibited widely across the South West and over the past five years she has further developed her practice to include portraits. Her work has been published in national magazines and she has a regular photographic feature in the Somerset Magazine. The photographs in this book have been taken from a solo exhibition commissioned to mark the 800th anniversary of Bridgwater's original town charters. *Bridgwater – The Parrett's Mouth* is her first book.

James Crowden was born in 1954 and grew up on the western edge of Dartmoor. He joined the army, read civil engineering at Bristol University, and in 1976 hightailed it to the Himalayas. He studied anthropology at Oxford, and lived for a year in the Outer Hebrides, before returning to Bristol and working in the docks as a boatman. He also worked for twenty years as an agricultural labourer, doing sheep shearing, night lambing, forestry and cidermaking. He recently retired from the land to concentrate on writing full-time. His other books are *Blood, Earth and Medicine* (1991), a collection of poems ("Ted Hughes territory seen from the inside" – *Daily Telegraph*), *In Time of Flood – The Somerset Levels – The River Parrett* (1996), a collection of poems and notes with photographs by George Wright ("Enjoyed it. Full of interesting effects. Unexpected things" – Ted Hughes), and *Cider – The Forgotten Miracle* (1999), an account of cidermaking and its history ("Well researched" – *Financial Times*).